A BUSINESS APPROACH TO RASPBERRY FARMING

Complete Entrepreneurial Step By Step Guide To Raspberry Garden From Scratch

ZHURI HART

DISCLAIMER

This book is intended to provide general information and insights on adopting a business approach to farming. The content within is based on the author's knowledge and experiences up to the date of publication. It is essential to recognize that the field of agriculture is dynamic, influenced by various factors such as market conditions, climate, and regulatory changes.

Readers are advised to conduct thorough research, seek professional advice, and consider their unique circumstances before implementing any strategies or practices discussed in this book. The author and publisher disclaim any responsibility for the accuracy, completeness, or suitability of the information provided. The book is not a substitute for professional advice, and the author and publisher shall not be liable for any damages or losses arising from the use or reliance on the information presented herein.

Individual results may vary, and success in farming enterprises is contingent upon numerous variables. The author encourages readers to consult with relevant experts, agricultural extension services, and legal or financial professionals to tailor strategies to their specific needs and local conditions.

This book is not intended to be a comprehensive guide to all aspects of farming, and readers should exercise their judgment and discretion in applying the principles discussed. The author and publisher do not endorse any specific products, services, or companies mentioned in this book unless explicitly stated.

By reading this book, the reader acknowledges and accepts the inherent uncertainties in agricultural endeavors and agrees to use the information at their own risk.

TABLE OF CONTENTS

ABOUT THE BOOK

Offering a thorough overview of the complexities involved in starting and running a profitable raspberry farming business, "A Business Approach to Raspberry Farming" is a priceless tool for prospective and seasoned raspberry growers alike.

The book explores the crucial facets of raspberry farming from a strategic business standpoint, stressing the industry's financial sustainability.

By giving background information and clarifying the goal and scope of the book, the introduction sets the stage. It recognizes the value of raspberry growing in both domestic and international markets, highlighting its importance in the agricultural landscape.

The book's later sections are thoughtfully organized to lead readers through a methodical learning process. Understanding Raspberries delves into the several types of raspberries, their growth phases, and critical elements including soil composition, pest control, and climate. Making wise judgments at every stage of farming requires this fundamental understanding.

By examining consumer trends, market dynamics, and a comprehensive competitor study, Market Research and Trends delves into the commercial side of raspberry cultivation. Farmers can use this knowledge to strategically place their products and take advantage of new niche markets.

Planning Your Raspberry Farm involves a hands-on approach to risk management, budgeting, goal-setting, and business planning. These sections give readers a strong foundation for creating a financially stable and long-lasting raspberry farming operation.

Important areas that help farmers with the practical aspects of raspberry farming are Site Selection and Preparation, Planting and Cultivation Practices, and Integrated Pest and Disease Management. These chapters offer practical advice for successful growing, from picking the ideal spot to putting in place efficient pest control techniques.

The crucial stages of enjoying the rewards of labor—timing the harvest, using the right methods, and guaranteeing quality control in sorting, packing, and storage—are illuminated by harvesting and post-harvest handling.

The commercial aspect of raspberry farming is handled via financial management and marketing strategies. These parts stress the significance of building strong financial records, developing marketing strategies, and building a strong brand to guarantee the enterprise's long-term feasibility.

Scaling Your Raspberry Business offers advice on growing your business through diversification tactics, manufacturing expansion, and growth challenge management. The information in this part gives readers the tools they need to advance their raspberry growing efforts.

"A Business Approach to Raspberry Farming" is an essential read for anyone wishing to get into or advance in the raspberry farming sector.

The full range of raspberry production is covered by its methodical and strategic approach, which guarantees that readers will not only have the requisite agricultural knowledge but also the commercial acumen required for sustained success in this cutthroat industry.

CHAPTER ONE

RASPBERRY FARMING INTRODUCTION

CONTEXT

Because of the increased demand for these tasty and nourishing berries, raspberry farming has become a key area of horticulture in recent years. The origins of raspberry cultivation can be found in the raspberries' natural habitat, which is found in North America, Europe, and Asia. Raspberries are now grown all over the world, with many different kinds that are suited to different temperatures.

In addition to being a long-standing custom, raspberry cultivation is now a booming business. Raspberries were first collected in the wild, but as agricultural techniques improved, cultivation became more structured. Large- and small-scale raspberry farming activities are now common, adding to the agricultural diversity of many areas.

THE EXTENT AND SIGNIFICANCE OF FARMING RASPBERRIES

The production of fruit is not the only purpose of raspberry gardening. Raspberries are a fruit that can be used in many different industries, such as food processing, medicine, and cosmetics. Consequently, growing raspberries has turned into a profitable endeavor that draws interest from both farmers and businesspeople.

To maximize output and quality, cultivation techniques have also evolved, embracing contemporary technology and sustainable methods.

The nutritious value of raspberries is what makes them important for farming. Because of their abundance of vitamins, minerals, and antioxidants, raspberries are a great complement to any diet.

Raspberries are becoming more and more popular as a commodity on the international market due to the growing desire for natural and nutrient-dense foods.

Additionally, by generating revenue for farmers and opening up job opportunities, raspberry growing supports economic development. With continuous research focused on creating new varieties, refining cultivation techniques, and advancing post-harvest technologies, the industry has also emerged as a source of innovation.

In terms of its impact on the environment, raspberry growing helps to advance sustainable agriculture. To reduce the negative effects of farming on the environment, many farmers are implementing environmentally friendly techniques including integrated pest control and organic farming. This is in line with consumers' growing desire for food goods made sustainably.

The history of raspberry farming shows how it progressed from unorganized gathering to planned production. Raspberry farming covers a wide range of topics, such as growing methods, uses for raspberries, and developments in the sector.

Beyond its financial worth, raspberry farming is significant because it improves nutrition, health, and environmental sustainability. The market is set up for future growth and innovation as long as there is a need for raspberries.

CHAPTER TWO

COMPREHENDING RASPBERRIES

DIFFERENT TYPES OF RASPBERRIES

As members of the Rubus genus, raspberries come in a wide range of types, each with its distinct flavor, color, and size. Red raspberries (Rubus idaeus), one of the most popular cultivars, are prized for their vivid color and tart-sweet flavor.

Rubus occidentalis, or black raspberries, are another well-liked variety with a somewhat sweeter flavor profile and a distinctive dark color. There are also golden raspberries (Rubus idaeus var. aureus), which have a lighter yellow color and a softer flavor. Cultivators must select the appropriate variety according to their soil and environment since each one has a unique set of ideal growing circumstances.

STAGES OF DEVELOPMENT AND GROWTH

Raspberries go through numerous unique stages of growth and development, each of which is essential to the total production of the plant. The propagation of raspberry plants via seeds or vegetative techniques such as cuttings marks the beginning of the life cycle. Following establishment, the plants progress onto the vegetative growth stage, which is marked by the growth of stems and leaves?

The plants next enter the flowering stage, during which time tiny buds develop into exquisite white or pink blooms. Fruit creation starts after successful pollination, and berries progressively mature through color changes.

Ultimately, to prepare for the upcoming growth cycle, the plants go into dormancy throughout the winter. It is essential to comprehend and handle each step to maximize Raspberry output and quality.

CONDITIONS OF THE SOIL AND CLIMATE

Raspberries grow best in temperate regions with distinct seasons, and the amount of daylight and temperature affect their growth. While mild temperatures throughout the growing season encourage rapid development and fruiting, adequate chilling hours during the winter are necessary to break dormancy. Well-drained soil in the pH range of slightly acidic to neutral is preferred for raspberries. The best soil types to avoid soggy situations that can cause root illnesses are sandy loam or loamy soil types. A good environment for raspberry plants also includes well-prepared soil and the addition of organic matter. Making the right site selection and controlling the soil is essential to making raspberry growing successful.

MANAGEMENT OF DISEASES AND PESTS

The production and well-being of raspberry plants are contingent upon the implementation of efficient pest and disease control measures. Japanese beetles, spider mites, and aphids are common pests that affect raspberries. By using integrated pest management techniques, such as beneficial insect release and routine monitoring, pest populations can be controlled without using excessive amounts of pesticides. Plants can be impacted by diseases such as powdery mildew, anthracnose, and raspberry cane blight, which calls for preventive actions such as correct spacing, trimming, and fungicide treatments. A thorough plan for managing pests and diseases must include both routine inspections and quick response when symptoms are noticed. Furthermore, preserving the general health of the plant with appropriate cultural techniques increases raspberries' resistance to certain dangers.

CHAPTER THREE

TRENDS AND MARKET RESEARCH

OVERVIEW OF THE MARKET

A comprehensive insight into the market's developments and the current situation is offered by the market overview. It includes an examination of several variables, including size, potential for growth, and important forces influencing the sector. The market overview for raspberry goods would focus on the unique trends and demands related to raspberries while delving into the broader fruit products industry. The purpose of this part is to lay the groundwork for future research into consumer trends, competitive analysis, and niche market identification by providing a fundamental grasp of the market landscape.

TRENDS IN RASPBERRY PRODUCT CONSUMPTION

Comprehending customer patterns is crucial for customizing items to accommodate changing tastes. There are a few major trends in raspberry products. There is a growing trend among customers to choose natural and organic foods, as well as healthier options. Due to their high vitamin and antioxidant content, raspberries fit in nicely with this movement for better health.

In addition, there is a growing market for creative and practical raspberry-based goods, like drinks, sweets, and snacks. Customers are also influenced by the emphasis on sustainability and ethical sourcing to choose businesses that use ecologically friendly methods in the manufacturing and cultivation of raspberries.

ANALYSIS OF COMPETITORS

For companies looking to get a competitive advantage in the market, a comprehensive competitor study is crucial. This entails evaluating the advantages and disadvantages of the current raspberry product market participants.

Product portfolios, pricing schemes, distribution routes, and marketing tactics are all examined.

Businesses can improve their strategies and set themselves apart from the competition by pinpointing their main rivals and researching their market positioning. Businesses may develop and adapt thanks to this competitive intelligence, remaining sensitive to shifting consumer tastes and market dynamics.

FINDING SPECIALIZED MARKETS

Finding underdeveloped market segments with particular demands or preferences is the first step in identifying niche markets. Potential markets for raspberry products could be specific applications or distinctive product formulas.

For example, a market for high-end, handcrafted raspberry jams or skincare products infused with raspberries, making use of the fruit's antioxidant qualities, may be expanding. Businesses can create goods that specifically address these wants by knowing these specialized markets, which will increase brand loyalty and provide them with a competitive edge. Finding niche markets is a calculated move that aims to both satisfy current demands and foresee and develop future market trends.

CHAPTER FOUR

ORGANIZING YOUR FARM FOR RASPBERRIES

FUNDAMENTALS OF BUSINESS PLANNING

To achieve long-term success, starting a raspberry farm requires a strong foundation in business strategy. It is essential to create a thorough business strategy that describes the general goals and objectives of the farm before getting into the intricacies of cultivation and upkeep. A thorough grasp of the market, your target audience, and your raspberries' USP should all be included in this strategy. Determining possible rivals and evaluating industry patterns will assist in strategically placing your farm.

ESTABLISHING OBJECTIVES AND GOALS

Any agricultural enterprise must have well-defined and attainable objectives to be successful, and raspberry farms are no exception. Start by establishing both short- and long-term goals that complement your farm's overarching purpose. Take into account variables including the intended manufacturing scale, revenue goals, and market share. Objectives may also encompass sustainability and environmental concerns, endorsing conscientious and moral farming methods. Setting performance indicators will also enable you to monitor your progress and modify your plan of action as necessary.

FINANCIAL PLANNING AND BUDGETING

Planning a raspberry farm requires developing a reasonable budget. This entails calculating the price of purchasing land, building infrastructure, raising seedlings, hiring labor, purchasing equipment, and continuing operating expenditures. Make sure you do a comprehensive investigation to obtain precise pricing data and account for unforeseen costs.

Revenue estimates based on anticipated yields and market prices should also be included in financial planning. Finding sources of finance and looking into grants or subsidies can help the Raspberry Farm be financially stable.

RISK CONTROL

Raising raspberries sustainably requires a proactive approach to risk management because farming entails a variety of inherent risks. Determine possible hazards including erratic weather, insect infestations, and volatile markets. Create plans to reduce these risks, such as putting in weather-resistant infrastructure, controlling pests, and diversifying your crop portfolio to account for fluctuations in the market. To guard against unforeseen circumstances that can negatively affect the farm's financial stability, insurance coverage should be taken into consideration. Update and reevaluate the risk management strategy regularly to accommodate shifting agricultural conditions. All things considered, a well-planned risk management approach is essential to your raspberry farm's durability and resilience.

CHAPTER FIVE

CHOOSING AND SETTING UP THE SITE

SELECTING THE IDEAL SITE

Selecting an appropriate site for a project is a crucial choice that can greatly influence its outcome. It entails a careful examination of several variables, such as market demand, accessibility, closeness to resources, and regulatory concerns. Easy access to transportation networks—like highways, trains, and ports—is essential for facilitating the flow of people and products. Additionally, to guarantee the project's long-term success, it is crucial to comprehend the demographic and economic trends of the selected site.

TESTING AND MODIFICATIONS TO THE SOIL

An essential part of site preparation, especially for building or agricultural operations, is soil testing and amendments. Assessing the composition, fertility, and drainage properties of the soil is aided by performing a thorough soil study. This data is essential for assessing the soil's compatibility for the planned use and identifying any modifications that may be required. To improve fertility and structure, amendments can involve adding organic matter, fertilizers, or other soil conditioners. Early planning attention to soil concerns can help to avoid problems later on and increase the project's overall success.

INFRASTRUCTURE NEEDS

Essential factors to take into account when choosing and getting ready for a location are the infrastructure needs. For projects to run well, the current infrastructure must be evaluated or the necessity for additional facilities must be determined. Transportation facilities, waste management systems, telephone networks, and power supplies are examples of adequate infrastructure.

By assessing these factors, you may be confident the project will work well and adhere to the requirements.

Furthermore, taking future development and expansion plans into account aids in decision-making regarding the scope and capacity of the infrastructure that needs to be constructed.

WATER RESOURCES MANAGEMENT

One of the most important site preparation tasks is water management, which calls for meticulous planning and execution. Comprehending the origins, availability, and quality of water is crucial for the creation of sustainable projects. Creating systems for wastewater treatment, drainage, and water supply is an essential part of efficient water management.

This is particularly important in industries where water is a scarce resource or when appropriate use of water is required by environmental standards. Adopting efficient water management techniques promotes project sustainability over the long run and environmental preservation in addition to ensuring compliance.

A comprehensive strategy that takes into account several variables is employed during the site selection and preparation process. A project's success is largely dependent on its location, which should take accessibility, market dynamics, and legal requirements into account. Optimizing land usage requires soil testing and amendments, while water management and infrastructural requirements are critical to project operations and sustainable practices. To be successful in any endeavor, these ideas must be thoroughly understood and strategically considered.

CHAPTER SIX

TECHNIQUES FOR PLANTING AND CULTIVATION

METHODS OF PROPAGATION

Plant growth and agricultural cultivation need the use of propagation techniques. By using these techniques, plants can be reproduced using their natural structures, such as seeds, cuttings, or other plant parts. One popular technique for propagating plants is seed germination, in which seeds are sown in appropriate soil and, given the right amount of moisture and temperature, germinate and grow into new plants. This technique is used for a wide range of crops, including vegetables and cereals.

Another common method of multiplication is cuttings, especially for perennial plants like shrubs and flowers. This technique involves removing a section of the plant, like a stem or leaf, and putting it in a location that will encourage the growth of roots.

These cuttings can grow into separate plants while maintaining the genetic traits of the parent plant if given the right care.

PLANTING METHODS

Crop establishment and growth depend heavily on the use of efficient planting procedures. Plants placed appropriately help to maximize productivity and maximize the use of available resources. Crops planted in rows or straight lines are commonly planted because they make cultivation, irrigation, and harvesting easier. Large-scale agriculture frequently uses this technique for crops like corn and soybeans.

Another planting method that entails growing two or more crops concurrently on the same field is intercropping. By using this technique, you can lower the danger of pests and illnesses while also increasing biodiversity and soil health.

Additionally, because various crops may have complimentary growth patterns and nutritional requirements, intercropping enables the optimal use of resources and space.

SYSTEMS OF IRRIGATION

An essential part of planting and cultivating is irrigation, particularly in areas where rainfall is insufficient for healthy plant growth. A variety of irrigation techniques are used to guarantee a steady and sufficient supply of water for crops. For example, drip irrigation minimizes water waste and increases water-use efficiency by applying water to the plant's root zone gradually and precisely.

Furrow and flood irrigation are two types of surface irrigation that spread water across the soil's surface so that it can penetrate and feed the plants. Despite being easier to use and less expensive, these techniques could cause uneven distribution and water runoff, which would reduce crop uniformity.

Conversely, sprinkler systems can be used with a variety of crops and soil types since they distribute water over the crops in a manner that mimics natural rainfall.

METHODS OF FERTILIZATION

A crucial component of cultivation techniques is fertilization, which gives plants the nutrients they need for healthy growth and development. Various fertilization techniques are used depending on the type of crop, the state of the soil, and the need for particular nutrients. Compost and manure are examples of organic fertilizers that improve the nutrient content and soil structure, fostering the long-term health and sustainability of the soil.

For precise nutrition control, inorganic or synthetic fertilizers with predetermined ratios of vital nutrients are frequently utilized. With the use of these fertilizers, farmers can customize nutrient applications to meet the needs of various crops at different stages of growth.

CHAPTER SEVEN

COMBINING DISEASE AND PEST CONTROL

RECOGNIZING TYPICAL INSECTS AND ILLNESSES

The goal of integrated pest and disease management (IPDM), a comprehensive strategy, is to minimize the detrimental effects on the environment and public health while addressing the issues that pests and diseases present in agriculture. The identification of common agricultural pests and diseases is one of the core components of integrated pest management (IPDM).

This calls for a thorough study of the crop varieties, local environment, and prevailing meteorological circumstances. Through the identification of the particular pests and diseases that endanger crops, farmers can better customize their management approaches.

CONTROL AND PREVENTIVE ACTIONS

An essential part of IPDM is prevention and control strategies. Using proactive measures to reduce the likelihood of pest and disease infestations is known as prevention. Crop rotation, choosing resistant crop kinds, and upholding appropriate sanitation procedures are a few examples of these tactics. Conversely, control strategies concentrate on lessening the effects of illnesses and pests after they have been discovered. Conventional farming often uses chemical pesticides; however, IPDM promotes the careful and targeted application of these chemicals to protect non-target organisms and lessen environmental damage.

NATURAL SOLUTIONS FOR PEST MANAGEMENT

Organic pest management techniques are becoming more and more popular in the IPDM field as environmentally friendly substitutes for traditional chemical treatments. Using nematodes or other beneficial insects as natural predators to suppress pest populations is a key component of organic pest management. Furthermore, cultural methods like adding biodiversity and companion planting are essential to organic pest management. These techniques support the general resilience and health of the agroecosystem in addition to aiding in pest management.

Moreover, releasing predators or parasites to manage pest populations is a component of biological control techniques, which are a subset of organic pest management. This strategy takes advantage of the predatory interactions that exist between various creatures to capitalize on the natural equilibrium within ecosystems. In addition to providing an eco-friendly substitute, biological control techniques lessen the need for artificial pesticides, promoting sustainable farming methods.

IPDM acknowledges the significance of using diverse management approaches according to the unique circumstances of every farming system.

Farmers can reduce the risks associated with pests and illnesses by building a resilient and balanced agroecosystem by carefully combining cultural, biological, and chemical management methods. This integrated approach supports farming communities' well-being and long-term environmental sustainability in addition to increasing agricultural output.

CHAPTER EIGHT

HARVESTING AND HANDLING AFTER HARVEST

CHOOSING THE APPROPRIATE TIME TO HARVEST

A key element in guaranteeing the best possible crop output and quality is harvest scheduling. Farmers need to pay close attention to these cues, as different crops have distinct markers that indicate when they are ready for harvest. The maturity, size, texture, color changes, and other factors all play a major part in selecting when to harvest. Furthermore, climate and environmental factors can affect when crops are harvested because various crops have varying reactions to changes in temperature and precipitation.

Cutting-edge technologies, like sensors and imaging systems, are frequently used in modern agricultural techniques to monitor and evaluate crop development, helping farmers choose the best time to harvest their crops.

METHODS OF HARVESTING

The methods used for harvesting differ based on the crop type and its unique needs. Handheld tools and personnel are still used in the manual harvesting process for some crops, such as fruits and vegetables. On the other hand, mechanized harvesting uses equipment like combine harvesters to harvest grains on a huge scale. Harvesting processes have been further refined by precision agriculture technologies, such as GPS-guided equipment, which increase productivity while decreasing waste. The crop's delicate nature and vulnerability to harm should be carefully taken into account while choosing the best harvesting technique to optimize both overall output and quality.

PUTTING TOGETHER, STORING, AND PACKING

Crops go through several post-harvest procedures after harvest, such as sorting, packing, and storing. Sorting is dividing crops according to factors like size, ripeness, and quality to guarantee uniformity in the finished product. Packing techniques differ and are based on the crop's characteristics, the needs of the market, and the needs of transportation. For example, bigger crops might be better suited for larger containers, while delicate fruits might need specific packing to prevent bruising. Harvested crops must be stored properly to preserve their freshness and quality. To decrease post-harvest losses and increase the shelf life of perishable crops, common techniques include drying facilities, cold storage, and controlled atmosphere storage.

QUALITY ASSURANCE

A crucial component of the entire harvesting and post-harvest handling process is quality control. Strict quality controls aid in locating and removing flaws or abnormalities in the harvested produce. Visual inspections, sensory analyses, and, in certain situations, laboratory testing for particular characteristics like moisture content, sugar levels, or chemical composition are examples of quality control methods.

By putting quality control procedures into place, producers may build a solid reputation and increase consumer satisfaction by ensuring that only products that satisfy predetermined requirements enter the market. From harvest to distribution, there must be constant monitoring to reduce the possibility of spoiling, contamination, and financial losses. This will ultimately help to create a resilient and sustainable agricultural system.

CHAPTER NINE

ADVERTISING TECHNIQUES

PUTTING YOUR RASPBERRY COMPANY'S BRANDING TO USE

To provide your raspberry business with a unique character in the marketplace, branding is essential. It entails developing a distinctive and enduring image that distinguishes your company from rivals.

A strong brand should communicate your company's principles and character in addition to the quality and flavor of your raspberries. Think about creating an engaging brand narrative that tells the tale of your raspberries from farm to table and connects with consumers.

Customer loyalty and brand awareness are increased when a company's branding is consistent throughout its web presence, marketing collateral, and packaging.

FORMULATING A SUCCESSFUL MARKETING STRATEGY

A successful marketing strategy is necessary for any raspberry business to succeed. To begin with, thoroughly investigate the interests and behaviors of your target market through market research. Determine your USPs (unique selling points) and develop a communications plan that successfully conveys them.

Because there are many different ways that customers interact with information, your marketing strategy should incorporate both online and offline tactics. To obtain the most reach and impact, distribute your cash sensibly over a range of platforms, including social media, content marketing, and traditional advertising.

CHANNELS FOR ONLINE AND OFFLINE MARKETING

Reaching a larger audience in the digital age requires integrating offline and online marketing methods. Campaigns can be targeted and measured via online channels including social media, websites, and email marketing. Make the most of social media to interact with customers, present aesthetically pleasing content, and create a virtual community around your Raspberry brand. In addition, face-to-face contact through offline channels such as farmers' markets, festivals, and partnerships with nearby businesses promote a feeling of genuineness and confidence.

DEVELOPING CONNECTIONS WITH PURCHASERS

Establishing trusting bonds with customers is essential to maintaining a profitable raspberry business. Interact with your clients on social media by quickly answering their questions and providing feedback. A client loyalty program might be put in place to encourage recurring business and cultivate a feeling of gratitude.

Work along with wholesalers and retailers to make sure customers can easily obtain your raspberries. Furthermore, think about organizing workshops or events to establish a direct connection with your target market, impart useful knowledge about raspberries, and reaffirm your brand's dedication to excellence.

A comprehensive strategy that includes branding, strategic planning, a well-balanced combination of online and offline channels, and establishing enduring relationships with customers is necessary for effective marketing. Through careful consideration of these ideas, your Raspberry Company can make a name for itself and prosper in the cutthroat agriculture and food sector.

MONEY HANDLING

Effective accounting and record-keeping are essential components of every organization's sound financial management. Maintaining accurate and thorough records of a company's financial activity is possible through the methodical documentation of financial transactions.

Keeping track of income, expenses, assets, and liabilities requires the use of this procedure. Precise documentation not only guarantees adherence to legal mandates but also supports tactical choice-making by providing discernment into monetary trends and patterns. The classification, analysis, and interpretation of financial data are all part of accounting, which produces financial statements that show the state of the company's finances. Businesses can improve performance evaluation, promote stakeholder confidence, and increase responsibility by keeping clear and well-documented records.

Maintaining a balance between cash inflows and outflows is the basic goal of cash flow management, which is an essential component of financial management. It entails keeping an eye on, evaluating, and optimizing the flow of money inside an organization.

A negative cash flow can result in unstable finances, whereas a positive cash flow guarantees that the business has sufficient liquid assets to meet its obligations, including debt payments and operating costs. Accurate cash flow estimates, efficient receivables and payables management, and the creation of backup plans for unanticipated events are all necessary for effective cash flow management. Businesses can increase their financial resilience, take advantage of growth possibilities, and reduce the risks related to liquidity issues by maintaining a stable cash flow.

A thorough review of a business's capacity to turn a profit from its costs and investments is known as profitability analysis. It entails evaluating how well-suited different product lines, market niches, or company operations are to support total profitability. In profitability analysis, key financial ratios like return on investment, net profit margin, and gross profit margin are frequently utilized. Through the analysis of revenue streams and cost structures, companies can pinpoint opportunities for enhancement, streamline the distribution of resources, and arrive at well-informed strategic choices. Understanding a company's financial viability, luring investors, and directing long-term growth strategies all depend on profitability research.

SEEKING MONEY AND GRANTS

Securing money and grants is frequently a crucial step in the financial management process for companies looking to grow or for startups aiming for initial growth. This entails locating appropriate funding sources, such as grants from the government, debt finance, or equity investments, and crafting strong grant or investment bids to draw in possible backers. Companies must exhibit a thorough grasp of their financial requirements, a solid business plan, and an accurate estimate of their return on investment. Securing funds or grants also depends on the company's objective, vision, and potential impact being communicated clearly. In addition to providing the funds required for expansion, effective funding techniques build credibility and garner support from outside parties, which promotes long-term financial sustainability.

CHAPTER TEN

GROWING YOUR RASPBERRY ENTERPRISE

INCREASING OUTPUT

To scale your Raspberry business and satisfy the increasing demand for your products, you must first expand your production. This entails building up your production facilities' capacity, streamlining the manufacturing process, and making sure your supply chain is dependable. It's critical to evaluate present production capacities, pinpoint bottlenecks, and make investments in cutting-edge technologies to boost efficiency when thinking about scaling up. Furthermore, investigating joint ventures with distributors and suppliers might facilitate raw material acquisition and enhance the overall scalability of production. A deliberate approach is needed to scale production, one that strikes a balance between the demand for higher output and the preservation of operational excellence and product quality.

STRATEGIES FOR DIVERSIFICATION

To reduce risks and take advantage of new opportunities in the raspberry industry, diversification is essential. Go beyond just growing and selling raspberries and think about expanding your line of products. This can entail creating brand-new raspberry-based goods to appeal to various market niches, including jams, drinks, or snacks. Examining various offline and online distribution channels can also aid in growing your clientele. New revenue streams may also become available by branching out into similar markets or industries, like organic or specialized foods. Using diversification techniques can help your company become more resilient to external shocks and establish your brand as a flexible player in the marketplace.

HANDLING THE DIFFICULTIES OF GROWTH

To achieve sustainable growth, scaling a Raspberry business has several problems that must be successfully handled. Upholding industry standards and ensuring continuous quality while production rises is a major challenge. Investing in employee training and putting in place strict quality control procedures can assist overcome this issue. Another crucial component is managing cash flow, since quick expansion could call for large financial outlays. Navigating this difficulty requires developing good financial management habits, obtaining more financing if needed, and keeping a careful eye on spending. Keeping lines of communication open and cultivating a healthy work environment is also essential to coordinating your expanding workforce with the objectives of the business.

ECOLOGICAL METHODS

Embracing sustainable methods is crucial for your Raspberry business's long-term success and reputation when you pursue growth. Organic farming and water conservation are two examples of eco-friendly farming methods that not only encourage environmental stewardship but also appeal to a growing number of environmentally conscious consumers. Using energy-efficient solutions in your company's distribution and production processes can help you leave a smaller environmental impact. Furthermore, investigating waste reduction techniques and sustainable packaging solutions shows a dedication to environmental responsibility. Including sustainable practices in your business model can improve brand loyalty among customers who value making environmentally friendly decisions, in addition to being in line with current global trends.

www.ingramcontent.com/pod-product-compliance
Lightning Source LLC
Chambersburg PA
CBHW070822290526
45795CB00002B/818